D0407455

DATE DUE   SEP 0 5

FEB 27

GAYLORD   PRINTED IN U.S.A.

SandCastle 3

Homophones

Where Do I Wear Water Wings?

Mary Elizabeth Salzmann

Publishing Company

JACKSON COUNTY LIBRARY SERVICES
MEDFORD, OREGON 97501

Published by SandCastle™, an imprint of ABDO Publishing Company, 4940 Viking Drive, Edina, Minnesota 55435.

Cover and interior photo credits: Artville, Comstock, Corel, Diamar, Eyewire Images, PhotoDisc

Library of Congress Cataloging-in-Publication Data

Salzmann, Mary Elizabeth, 1968-
  Where do I wear water wings? / Mary Elizabeth Salzmann.
    p. cm. -- (Homophones)
  Includes index.
  Summary: Photographs and simple text introduce homophones, words that sound alike but are spelled differently and have different meanings.
  ISBN 1-57765-799-3
  1. English language--Homonyms--Juvenile literature. [1. English language--Homonyms.] I. Title. II. Series.

PE1595 .S28 2002
428.1--dc21
                                                          2001053307

The SandCastle concept, content, and reading method have been reviewed and approved by a national advisory board including literacy specialists, librarians, elementary school teachers, early childhood education professionals, and parents.

Let Us Know

After reading the book, SandCastle would like you to tell us your stories about reading. What is your favorite page? Was there something hard that you needed help with? Share the ups and downs of learning to read. We want to hear from you! To get posted on the ABDO Publishing Company Web site, send us email at:

sandcastle@abdopub.com

About SandCastle™
Nonfiction books for the beginning reader

- Basic concepts of phonics are incorporated with integrated language methods of reading instruction. Most words are short, and phrases, letter sounds, and word sounds are repeated.

- Book levels are based on the ATOS™ for Books formula. Other considerations for readability include the number of words in each sentence, the number of characters in each word, and word lists based on curriculum frameworks.

- Full-color photography reinforces word meanings and concepts.

- "Words I Can Read" list at the end of each book teaches basic elements of grammar, helps the reader recognize the words in the text, and builds vocabulary.

- Reading levels are indicated by the number of flags on the castle.

SandCastle uses the following definitions for this series:

- Homographs: words that are spelled the same but sound different and have different meanings. *Easy memory tip: "-graph"= same look*

- Homonyms: words that are spelled and sound the same but have different meanings. *Easy memory tip: "-nym"= same name*

- Homophones: words that sound alike but are spelled differently and have different meanings. *Easy memory tip: "-phone"= sound alike*

Look for more SandCastle books in these three reading levels:

Level 1 (one flag)	**Level 2** (two flags)	**Level 3** (three flags)

Grades Pre-K to K 5 or fewer words per page	**Grades K to 1** 5 to 10 words per page	**Grades 1 to 2** 10 to 15 words per page

Note: Some pages in this book contain more than 15 words in order to more clearly convey the concept of the book.

where

a word used to ask
about the location
of something

wear

to be dressed
in something

Homophones are words that sound alike but are spelled differently and have different meanings.

Where do I find clothes to dress up in?

I find them in the attic.

This is my favorite cap.

I like to wear it backwards.

Where do I go to fish?

I go fishing at the lake.

Our dresses are alike.

We wear them for special holidays.

Where do we eat our snack?

We eat it in our tent.

I wear my red and white uniform when I play baseball.

Where did we go on our trip?

We went to the ocean.

I **wear** a special hat and jacket when I ride my horse.

Where do I play with my yellow duck?

I play with it in the pool.

I **wear** pink hair clips to match my pink shirt.

Where are we reading?

We are reading in the park.

We wear life vests when we go for a ride in our boat.

Where am I playing with my baby brother?

We are playing in the kitchen.

We **wear** funny masks.

No one can see what we really look like.

Where do I make sand castles?

I make sand castles at the beach.

What do I **wear** on my hands
when I work in the garden?
(gloves)

Words I Can Read

Nouns

A noun is a person, place, or thing

attic (AT-ik) p. 6

baseball (BAYSS-bawl)
  p. 11

beach (BEECH) p. 20

boat (BOTE) p. 17

brother (BRUHTH-ur)
  p. 18

cap (KAP) p. 7

clips (KLIPSS) p. 15

clothes (KLOHZ) p. 6

dresses (DRESS-ez)
  p. 9

duck (DUHK) p. 14

garden (GARD-uhn)
  p. 21

gloves (GLUHVZ) p. 21

hair (HAIR) p. 15

hands (HANDZ) p. 21

hat (HAT) p. 13

holidays
  (HOL-uh-dayz) p. 9

homophones
  (HOME-uh-fonez)
  p. 5

horse (HORSS) p. 13

jacket (JAK-it) p. 13

kitchen (KICH-uhn)
  p. 18

lake (LAKE) p. 8

life vests
  (LIFE VESTSS) p. 17

location
  (loh-KAY-shuhn) p. 4

masks (MASKSS) p. 19

meanings (MEE-ningz)
  p. 5

ocean (OH-shuhn)
  p. 12

park (PARK) p. 16

pool (POOL) p. 14

ride (RIDE) p. 17

sand castles
  (SAND KASS-uhlz)
  p. 20

shirt (SHURT) p. 15

snack (SNAK) p. 10

tent (TENT) p. 10

trip (TRIP) p. 12

uniform
  (YOO-nuh-form) p. 11

word (WURD) p. 4

words (WURDZ) p. 5

Pronouns

A pronoun is a word that replaces a noun

I (EYE) pp. 6, 7, 8, 11, 13, 14, 15, 18, 20, 21

it (IT) pp. 7, 10, 14

no one (NOH WUHN) p. 19

something (SUHM-thing) p. 4

them (THEM) pp. 6, 9

this (THISS) p. 7

we (WEE) pp. 9, 10, 12, 16, 17, 18, 19

what (WUHT) pp. 19, 21

Verbs

A verb is an action or being word

am (AM) p. 18

are (AR) pp. 5, 9, 16, 18

ask (ASK) p. 4

be (BEE) p. 4

can (KAN) p. 19

did (DID) p. 12

do (DOO) pp. 6, 8, 10, 14, 20, 21

dress up (DRESS UHP) p. 6

dressed (DRESSD) p. 4

eat (EET) p. 10

find (FINDE) p. 6

fish (FISH) p. 8

fishing (FISH-ing) p. 8

go (GOH) pp. 8, 12, 17

have (HAV) p. 5

is (IZ) p. 7

like (LIKE) p. 7

look (LUK) p. 19

make (MAKE) p. 20

match (MACH) p. 15

play (PLAY) pp. 11, 14

playing (PLAY-ing) p. 18

reading (REED-ing) p. 16

ride (RIDE) p. 13

see (SEE) p. 19

sound (SOUND) p. 5

spelled (SPELD) p. 5

used (YOOZD) p. 4

wear (WAIR) pp. 4, 7, 9, 11, 13, 15, 17, 19, 21

went (WENT) p. 12

work (WURK) p. 21

23

Adjectives

An adjective describes something

alike (uh-LIKE) pp. 5, 9
baby (BAY-bee) p. 18
different (DIF-ur-uhnt)
   p. 5
favorite (FAY-vuh-rit)
   p. 7

funny (FUH-nee) p. 19
my (MYE) pp. 7, 11, 13,
   14, 15, 18, 21
our (OUR)
   pp. 9, 10, 12, 17
pink (PINGK) p. 15

red (RED) p. 11
special (SPESH-uhl)
   pp. 9, 13
white (WITE) p. 11
yellow (YEL-oh) p. 14

Adverbs

An adverb tells how, when, or where something happens

backwards
  (BAK-wurdz) p. 7

differently
  (DIF-ur-uhnt-lee) p. 5
really (REE-lee) p. 19

where (WAIR) pp. 4, 6,
8, 10, 12, 14, 16, 18, 20